fast
fun &
eas

CHRISTMAS STOCKING

Festive Fabric Projects to S
Your Imaginati

Susan S. Te

C&T PUBLISHING

xt © 2005 Susan S. Terry

rtwork © 2005 C&T Publishing

ublisher: Amy Marson

ditorial Director: Gailen Runge

cquisitions Editor: Jan Grigsby

ditor: Lee Jonsson

echnical Editor: Franki Kohler

opyeditor/Proofreader: Wordfirm Inc.

over Designer/Book Designer: Kristy Zacharias

age Layout Artist: Kirstie L. McCormick

omposition Services: Happenstance Type-O-Rama

ustrator: Shawn Garcia, Kerry Graham

roduction Assistants: Kerry Graham, Kiera Lofgreen

hotography: Diane Pedersen, Luke Mulks, and Kirstie L.

McCormick unless otherwise noted

ublished by C&T Publishing, Inc., P.O. Box 1456, Lafayette,
alifornia, 94549

ll rights reserved. No part of this work covered by the
opyright hereon may be reproduced or used in any form
r any means—graphic, electronic, or mechanical, including
hotocopying, recording, taping, or information storage
nd retrieval systems—without written permission of the
ublisher. The copyrights on individual artworks are
etained by the artists as noted in *fast, fun & easy
Christmas Stockings.*

ttention Copy Shops: Please note the following exception—
ublisher and author give permission to photocopy pullout
or personal use only.

ttention Teachers: C&T Publishing, Inc. encourages you to
se this book as a text for teaching. Contact us at 800-284-
114 or www.ctpub.com for more information about the
C&T Teachers Program.

We take great care to ensure that the information included
n this book is accurate and presented in good faith, but no
varranty is provided nor results guaranteed. Having no
ontrol over the choices of materials or procedures used,
either the author nor C&T Publishing, Inc. shall have any
iability to any person or entity with respect to any loss or
damage caused directly or indirectly by the information
ontained in this book. For your convenience, we post an
up-to-date listing of corrections on our website
www.ctpub.com). If a correction is not already noted,
please contact our customer service department at
ctinfo@ctpub.com or at P.O. Box 1456, Lafayette, California,
94549.

Trademark (™) and registered trademark (®) names are
used throughout this book. Rather than use the symbols
with every occurrence of a trademark or registered trademark name, we are using the names only in the editorial
fashion and to the benefit of the owner, with no intention of
nfringement.

Library of Congress Cataloging-in-Publication Data

Terry, Susan S.,

Fast, fun & easy Christmas stockings: festive fabric projects
to stir your imagination / Susan S. Terry.

p. cm.

ISBN 1-57120-305-2 (paper trade)

1. Christmas stockings. I. Title.

TT900.C4T47 2005

745.594'12–dc22

2005003375

Printed in China

10 9 8 7 6 5 4 3 2 1

Dedication

In memory of my mother, Jean H. Spangenberg, who taught me to sew and to save.

Acknowledgments

My greatest thanks to my husband, Brent, who gives me the support and time I need to do the things I love.

I want to thank my friend and technical editor, Franki Kohler, for her encouragement in this endeavor. She was certain I could do it when I was sure I couldn't.

Early in my quilting career, I ran across a quilt by Florence Renli. With some finagling, I got her address in South Dakota and wrote to her with the many questions I had regarding her techniques. She took the time to write to me and, as a bonus, introduced me to her daughters, Aileyn Ecob and Jean Jurgenson, and her granddaughter Lee Jonsson; this is a very talented family of quilters. With their prompting, I joined a guild and met other quilters, and the rest is history. Thanks, gang.

Because I must have done *something* right in a previous life, Lee Jonsson was given the job of editing this book. My thanks to her and to all the staff at C&T Publishing who saw the project through.

And finally, I want to mention my monthly quilting group, The Not Ready for Prime Time Quilters: Jan Dodge, Bonnie Gronner, Nancy Hofer, Pat Hunt, Marilyn Hunt, Ann Jones, Marge Moran, and Rosamaria Wellman. First comes lunch and laughter; then, if we get around to it, we quilt.

Contents

Everybody Needs a Christmas Stocking: An Introduction

The women in my family have a Christmas stocking history.

In 1942, my grandmother gave me a Christmas stocking. It was very simply made from a piece of flannel and had my name and the year on it. It was my second Christmas and I already had a younger sister. She received a stocking too. Grandma went on to give each of her eleven grandchildren stockings. I still have mine.

After I presented my mother with her first grandchild, she began to knit Christmas stockings. She ultimately knitted each of her seven grandchildren a different stocking. Now when holiday time arrives, the stockings come out of storage and everyone remembers Grandma.

When my own grandchildren and grandnieces began to arrive, I decided to design and sew each one a quilt. However, I appliqué and quilt by hand, so I soon fell hopelessly behind schedule, sometimes as much as three years! I needed a quicker way to say, "Welcome."

One day, while I was eyeing my boxes of fabric scraps and casting around for a way to use them, Christmas stockings popped into my mind. "Of course, Christmas stockings! Fast, fun, and easy." I could use my scraps, dabble in design, play with machine appliqué, reduce my fabric stash, and sew something without having to quilt it. And maybe, after I had all this fun, the recipients of my stockings would remember me in some distant place and time.

Stepping Out: Basic Information and Techniques

Christmas in July: Choosing Fabrics

Stocking fabrics

When the Christmas fabrics arrive in the stores in late summer, I go shopping. I'm hoping to fall in love with a fabric and use it as inspiration for a stocking design. If I'm lucky enough to have a design in mind, I want to find the fabric that best suits it. Well, yes, I do have lots of choices already in my possession, but I wouldn't want to miss out on anything!

Before I understood the value of having a fabric stash, I'd find a great Christmas fabric at the store and then go home to think up a project that would justify its purchase. By the time I had managed to dream one up, smarter shoppers than I had done the *carpe diem* thing and I was out of luck. Now I buy it when I see it.

I often make Christmas stockings without using any Christmas fabrics. For these, I can shop all year. I look for red and green fabrics with gold or silver metallic stripes or threads, in geometric designs, plaids, checks, or dots. I buy dark blue fabrics with gold or silver stars, dots, or spirals; they are perfect to use as a night sky—and never go out of season. I also look for the lamés and sequined materials that give a stocking sparkle.

fun!

Make the same design two or three times to see how changing the background fabric changes the look of the stocking. This is good practice for putting colors together, and you can always find a recipient who will love a new Christmas stocking!

easy!

If you have trouble choosing the background fabric from all the choices at hand, make the stocking front from one fabric and the stocking back from another.

Using Scraps

In addition to a fabric stash, I have a scrap stash. In fact, I have several, sorted by size. I depend on scraps for both inspiration and execution of designs. Not only do I have "legitimate" scraps—leftovers accumulated from actual projects—but for variety, I also often take 6-inch cuts off the fabrics in my stash and throw these into the mix.

For all the projects, when minimal amounts of fabric are required, ⅛ yards are included in the materials list. This is code for: "If you have either scraps or a stash, you have this covered." If you don't have scraps, buy the minimal amounts, make your project, and then you *will* have scraps.

About the Projects

The simplest patterns in the book are the *Banner Stockings* (pages 13–17) and the *Poinsettia Stocking* (pages 18–20), which are made with one-piece back-grounds. The *"Santa's Been Here" Stocking* (pages 21–24) and the *Partridge Stocking* (pages 25–27) have paper-pieced backgrounds but can be made with one-piece backgrounds. The *Patchwork Stock-ing* (pages 28–31) uses traditional piecing methods, but the design looks best if you *don't* match the seams. For the *"Santa's Been Here" Stocking* and the *Patchwork Stockings*, as well as the miniature *Stockings for Elves* (pages 32–37), the simplest appliqué elements can be cut freehand, a fun and easy approach that individualizes the stocking you make. If you like, you can also use the patterns pro-vided on the pullout at the back of the book.

About the Pattern

My stockings began with a pattern I drew on a brown paper bag. As I made one and then another, I named each section of the pattern, standardized measurements, and streamlined construction.

The assembly technique I use lends itself to easily changing the basics. As you work with the pattern, you'll see that you can alter the size of the header or leave it off, eliminate the divider strip or resize it, or completely redraw the shape of the stocking.

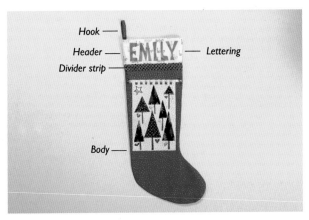

Stocking components

Stocking Basics

body

The fabric you choose for the stocking body will set the stage for the rest of the color and design scheme. I often choose the colors or theme by considering the recipient. I decide whether the colors should be bright and bold or subtle and muted...whether the design should be playful and whimsical or sophisti-cated and elegant. Once you decide on the overall color and design scheme, you will be able to make choices about the other elements.

header

The front header is where you'll put the stocking recipient's name. I try to find a fabric that in some way complements what I'm using for the stocking body. A strong contrast with the stocking body gives a different feel than a more subtle contrast.

lettering

The lettering fabric needs enough contrast with the header to allow the name to be easily read. If you use a plaid or print fabric for the header, you'll need a solid fabric for the lettering. For really glitzy let-ters, try lamé.

fun!

> Put the year on the back header of the stocking. For a future admirer of your work, this will help identify the "vintage."

divider strip

The divider strip separates the stocking header and body. Use a glittery lamé or sequined fabric to add a festive look.

stocking hook

Use scraps of background or header fabric to create the hook. It can be cut on the straight grain or on the bias.

Haven't got a place to hang a stocking? Buy over-the-door hooks and hang stockings throughout the house. They make wonderful Christmas decorations.

lining

For the lining, you could use some of that Christmas fabric you have on hand. Whatever you choose, decide on a color that goes well with the stocking body.

stabilizer

Use a stabilizer to provide a solid base for the decorative sewing and to add body to the stocking. Look for a medium-weight woven or nonwoven interfacing. Another choice is Pellon fleece, which gives a plumper feel to the finished stocking.

paper-backed fusible web

Use paper-backed fusible web to apply the appliqué designs and lettering. There are many brands available. While I've experimented with several fusibles, I still prefer Pellon Wonder-Under. Whatever you choose, follow the manufacturer's instructions for pressing.

Except where otherwise indicated, use this method in making the appliqué: Trace your pattern onto the paper side of the fusible web and cut it out, leaving a ¼-inch margin all around. Press the paper-backed fusible web to the wrong side of your fabric, then cut out the appliqué on the drawn line.

permanent pen

To make the "Merry Christmas" signs for the *"Santa's Been Here" Stocking* or to make labels, you need a permanent pen. For small writing, I generally use Pigma micron pens .01 to .05 (finer print to bolder print). If I plan on using a very bold script, I use a Sharpie Ultra-Fine Point pen. After using any permanent pen, the fabric must be pressed to ensure the ink's permanence.

Getting Organized

To make a stocking, choose a project and add the requirements of that project to the list below.

supply list

Stocking body fabric: 1 fat quarter
Stocking header fabric: ⅛ yard
Sequined fabric: ⅛ yard
Lettering fabric: ⅛ yard
Stocking lining: ⅔ yard
Stabilizer: ½ yard
Paper-backed fusible web: ½ yard
Pattern paper: ½ yard
Metallic gold thread

tools

General tools needed

General sewing supplies: fabric scissors, pins, seam ripper, small pointed scissors
Sewing machine

Metallic sewing machine needles

Sewing thread to match stocking fabric

Superior "Glitter" thread or Sulky Holoshimmer thread in a gold tone

Ironing board and iron

Rotary cutter and mat

Clear ruler, 6″ × 12″

Pressing cloth (or use an old handkerchief)

Scribbles paints (I find "Glittering Gold" to be the most useful.)

Good-quality tweezers and reverse tweezers (Find these at craft, fabric, or medical supply stores.)

Pattern paper (Find this at fabric stores.)

fast!

Working with small pieces is easy with tweezers. Once you're in the habit of using these, you'll feel shorthanded without them.

Basic Techniques

create the pattern

Using the patterns on the pullout at the back of the book, trace the stocking body onto pattern paper. Then trace the header pattern. Cut them out. Seam allowances are included in the pattern.

fun!

If you really want to go all out, make a stocking that can be turned either way. Decorate both sides differently and put the recipient's name on both the front and back header.

seam allowance

Use a ¼-inch seam allowance unless otherwise noted. Don't forget to allow for this allowance along the stocking edges and top when placing appliqués.

pressing

Read and follow the instructions that come with your paper-backed fusible web. *Be sure to use a pressing cloth when pressing lamé and sequined fabrics.*

alphabets and numbers

The alphabet and number set are reversed so that they can be copied directly onto the paper-backed fusible web.

Scribbles paints

One of my favorite ways to put sparkle into a stocking is with Scribbles, a three-dimensional fabric paint that comes in a little bottle with an applicator tip. If you've never used these paints, some practice is in order. Take a scrap of white fabric and, with a pencil, doodle a few hearts or stars or large letters on it. Before starting to paint on your fabric, pinch the bottle on a piece of scrap paper to start the paint flowing. Once you've "primed" the bottle, touch the tip of the Scribbles applicator lightly to the surface of the fabric, squeeze the bottle with an even pressure, and move it over the design at a steady speed. To end, lift the bottle quickly. You'll soon get the hang of it.

Using Scribbles paint

Keep a toothpick and a rag on hand when painting with Scribbles for what I call a "9-1-1." If too much paint gets on the fabric, *quickly* scrape the excess off with a toothpick and clean the toothpick with the rag. It often takes me several rescues to get it right.

When the painting is finished, the effort looks blobby and colorless. Not to worry—you'll love it when it's dry. Carefully put the stocking in a safe place and don't even *think* about picking it up again for at least four hours.

Using Scribbles will not only add color, but will also prevent the edges of the appliqués from raveling. When pressing a Scribbles design, use a pressing cloth.

labels

Why create a delightful stocking and not identify yourself as the maker? Fabric stores can order labels with your name, or if you want more than that on a label, "Santa, Who Are You? Making Labels" on pages 38–40 offers ideas and instructions for making your own.

making bows

Several of the stocking designs require bows. Here are four ways to make them.

Fabric Bows

1. Fuse paper-backed fusible web to the wrong side of a scrap of fabric.

2. Cut a wide triangle from it. Cut a "V" in the long edge of the triangle. Leave the top of the bow straight or cut both sides on an angle. Press the bow into place on the stocking.

Cut a "V" in long edge of triangle.

Leave top straight or cut on an angle.

Ribbon Bows

1. Cut a 6˝ piece of ⅛˝ ribbon. Skip the initial knot made when tying a shoe bow and start with the loops. Tie the bow and adjust the size to suit the design.

2. Thread a needle with a color that matches the bow and tie a knot in the thread. Come up through the back of the stocking and through the bow knot. Taking a *very* tiny stitch, go through the knot to the back of the stocking.

3. Repeat this several times, making sure that when the ends of the bow are tugged, they won't pull out. Tie off the thread and trim the ends of the bow.

easy!

If the ends of the bow look like they may ravel, put Fray Check on them. If the ends of the bow go off at an angle you don't like, position them the way you want them and glue them to the stocking with fabric glue.

Thread Bows

Coats and Clark metallic thread is my choice for making this bow, but you can also make it from other metallic thread or regular sewing thread.

1. Cut about a yard of thread off the spool. Then cut an 8˝ piece from the spool. Take the long piece, put the ends together, and fold it in half. Do this three times, until the bow is approximately 2¼˝ long. For a smaller bow, cut a shorter piece of thread; for a larger bow, cut a longer piece of thread.

2. Use the reverse tweezers to hold the folds of the thread in place.

3. Loop the shorter thread around the center of the folded threads and tie it tight.

4. Attach the bow by taking the ends of the center tie and running them through to the back of the stocking. Tack these down and fluff the bow into an attractive shape.

Tie loop around folded thread.

Curlicue Thread Bows

I've experimented with this bow using different types of metallic thread. When I don't use Superior "Glitter" or Sulky Holoshimmer thread, I don't get the tight curlicues I need for this bow.

1. Thread the machine with the metallic thread and tighten the tension. Grasp the thread as it comes through the needle and quickly pull off 9″– 12″ inches of thread. The thread will make curlicues. Cut off any part of the thread that's straight.

2. Cut several more pieces the same way. Scrunch and fold the curled thread together into a small ball. Hold it in place with reverse tweezers.

3. Lay the reverse tweezers on the project where you want the bow to be. Use several pins to pin the bow down. Remove the tweezers.

4. Thread a needle with a piece of the metallic thread and knot the end. With the needle, come up through the back of the stocking and run the thread

over the bow and back through the stocking, removing the pins as you stitch. Do this as many times as it takes to hold the curlicues in place.

5. Tie off the thread on the back of the stocking.

Curlicue thread bow in progress

hanging loops

Several stockings have hearts or other decorations appliquéd at the bottom of a tree. To make them seem as if they are hanging on the tree, thread a needle with metallic thread, double it, and make a knot. Come up through the top of the decoration or the "V" of the heart and go down just at the bottom edge of the tree, leaving the doubled thread with a tiny amount of slack on the front of the stocking. Tack the thread down on the back of the stocking.

Slack thread creates the illusion of hanging.

paper piecing

Some of the projects in the book are paper pieced. For these, refer to the following instructions.

1. Trace or photocopy the paper-piecing pattern. Firmly fold the pattern along *all* of the lines before starting.

2. Using a small stitch length (#1.5–1.8, or 18–20 stitches per inch), sew on the side of the paper with the lines. When stitching the line between pattern areas, start ¼″ before the start of the line and end ¼″ beyond the end of it.

3. Pieces do not need to be perfect shapes and you don't have to worry about the grain of the fabric, but it's a *very* good idea to cut each piece at least ¾″ larger all around than you think necessary. I'd rather waste small amounts of fabric than waste the time it takes to rip out all those tiny stitches.

4. Follow the number sequence when piecing. Pin piece #1 in place, right side of the fabric up on the side of the paper without the lines. Don't put the pin on the seamline. Hold the paper up to the light to be sure the piece covers area #1, with generous seam allowances overlapping the lines.

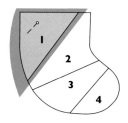

5. Fold the pattern back at the stitching line between the #1 and #2 areas. (You are reversing the fold you made in Step 1, folding the unmarked side of the pattern over the marked side.) Trim the fabric to a ¼″ seam allowance with a ruler and rotary cutter. Unfold the paper pattern.

6. Cut piece #2 large enough to cover the #2 area with a generous seam allowance. Align the edge with the trimmed seam allowance of piece #1, right sides together, and pin. Turn the paper over so that you can see the stitch line between areas #1 and #2 and stitch on this line.

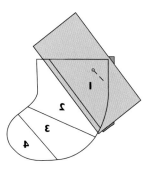

7. Open piece #2 and press.

8. Repeat Steps 5 and 6 for each piece, working in numerical order.

9. Don't trim the piece and don't take the paper off until you read the instructions in your project.

PAPER-PIECING HINT

When piecing a dark and a light fabric together where the seam allowance needs to be pressed toward the light fabric, the edge of the dark seam allowance will sometimes show through the light fabric. To prevent this, trim the dark seam allowance about 1⁄16″ narrower than the light seam allowance.

banner stockings

This type of stocking was the easy alternative to that Christmas banner I always meant to make. The stocking decoration is put on a rectangular background (a "banner") and then the banner is put on the stocking with a "rod." Choose contrasting fabrics for the banner and background fabrics.

Tree Banner Stocking,
made for Brent Terry,
2004

Angel Banner Stocking,
made for Bethann
Spangenberg, 2004

What You'll Need

Trees and angel wings are made from the ⅛ yard of sequined fabric called for in the main supply list. Refer to the main supply list on page 8 for the basics and add the following:

For either stocking:

- ☐ Gold lamé: ⅛ yard*
- ☐ Banner fabric: ¼ yard
- ☐ Finials on banner rod: 2 decorative buttons

For the tree banner:

- ☐ Green for trees: ⅛ yard*
- ☐ Brown/black for tree trunks: ⅛ yard*
- ☐ Red lamé: ⅛ yard*

For the angel banner:

- ☐ Flesh-colored fabric for the face: ⅛ yard*
- ☐ Fabric for the angel's dress: Scraps for paper piecing
- ☐ Angel's hair: 1 package of "Wild Hairs" or "Loopy Loops," available at craft stores
- ☐ Permanent pens: 1 red and 1 black
- ☐ Glue gun
- ☐ ⅛″-wide ribbon for a bow: 6″

*Remember! Use your stash of scraps wherever ⅛-yard requirements are listed.

How-Tos

cutting

1. Refer to "Create the Pattern" on page 9 and follow the instructions.

2. Fold the fat-quarter background in half and place it on a single layer of stabilizer. Pin the stocking pattern on top and cut it out.

3. Cut a 5½˝ × 8½˝ rectangle each from the banner fabric and the stabilizer for the banner.

easy!

If you're having placement trouble, use a Sharpie pen to trace the banner pattern onto a 5˝ × 8˝ piece of tissue paper. If you're using a light-colored fabric for the banner, put this pattern under the banner. If you're using a dark fabric for the banner, put the pattern over the banner piece.

tree banner

Use the following instructions for the tree banner.

tree banner appliqués

Refer to page 8 for instructions on using paper-backed fusible web. *Don't forget your pressing cloth.*

Use the pattern on the pullout at the back of the book. Be sure to include the pattern letters when tracing. Trace and fuse the pattern pieces onto paper-backed fusible web in the following groups:

1. Trace trees A, C, and E and fuse them to the sequined fabric.

2. Trace trees B, D, F, and G and fuse them to the tree fabric.

3. Trace the tree trunks and fuse them to the tree trunk fabric.

4. Trace 4 hearts and the star and fuse them to the gold lamé.

5. Trace 3 hearts and fuse them to the red lamé.

6. Cut out all the appliqués on the pattern lines.

easy!

Instead of using fabric for the tree trunks, use a satin stitch to create them.

fast!

Cut loose and draw or cut the hearts freehand. Asymmetrical designs are more interesting.

tree banner construction

1. Place the banner on the ironing board. Referring to the pattern, place the trees on the banner and slip the tops of the trunks under each tree. Place the hearts. With a ruler, check to be sure the appliqués are at least ¼˝ from the side or bottom edges of the banner and at least ⅝˝ from the top. When the positioning looks right, press everything into place.

2. Place the 5½˝ × 8½˝ piece of stabilizer on the wrong side of the banner and pin it in place. With metallic thread, machine stitch along the very edge of the trunks and trees using a straight stitch.

3. Refer to "Add the Banner to the Stocking" on page 16.

angel banner

Use the following instructions for the angel banner.

Paper Piecing the Dress

Refer to "Paper Piecing" on page 12 for complete instructions.

Copy the paper-piecing pattern on the pullout at the back of the book. Use this to piece green, gold, and red scraps into a 3½″ × 5″ rectangle. Don't trim the edges, but do remove the paper.

angel banner appliqués

Refer to page 8 for instructions on using paper-backed fusible web. *Don't forget your pressing cloth.*

Trace the patterns on the pullout at the back of the book onto fusible web.

1. Cut out the dress and fuse it to the paper-pieced angel dress fabric.

2. Cut out the wing and fuse it to the sequined fabric.

3. Cut out the arms and fuse them to a scrap of fabric that contrasts with the dress.

4. Cut out the face and fuse it to the face fabric.

5. Cut out the halo and heart and fuse them to the gold lamé.

6. Cut out all the appliqués on the pattern lines.

fast!

If you don't want to paper piece the angel's dress, make it from one piece of fabric.

angel banner construction

1. Use black permanent pen to draw the eyes and red permanent pen to draw the mouth on the angel's face. Refer to the pattern on the pullout at the back of the book.

2. Place the banner on the ironing board. Referring to the angel pattern, place the pieces on the banner in this order: wings, halo, dress, head, arms, and heart. The angel should be centered between the right and left edges of the banner, 1″ from the top of the banner and ½″ from the bottom. When you are satisfied with the placement, press the angel into place.

3. Pin the 5½″ × 8½″ piece of stabilizer to the wrong side of the banner. Use a straight stitch and metallic thread to machine stitch along the very edge of the halo, dress, arms, and wings.

add the banner to the stocking

1. Trim as much stabilizer as you can from the banner so the fusible web will adhere to the back of the banner.

2. Trace the banner pattern onto paper-backed fusible web and cut it out, leaving a ¼″ allowance. Center and fuse this to the back of the decorated banner. Cut out the banner on the lines.

fun!

Design your own banner stocking. Look for Christmas motifs in cards and gift wrap.

3. Cut a ½″ × 6½″ piece of paper-backed fusible web and fuse it to the gold lamé. From this, cut a ¼″ × 6″ piece for the banner rod.

4. On a banner stocking, the toe can point in either direction. Pull out the stocking body piece you want and center the banner rod 1¼″ down from the top of the body. Press the rod into place.

5. Pin the stabilizer to the stocking back.

6. Sew around the banner rod using metallic thread and a straight machine stitch.

fun!

Before pressing the banner onto the stocking, pink the bottom edge or sew a trimming onto it.

7. Center the bottom edge of the banner between the two sides of the stocking. Place the top of the banner just at the top of the rod, as if the banner were hanging on it, and press it into place. Sew around the entire edge of the banner.

8. Sew a button over each end of the rod. For ease in sewing the stocking together, don't extend the button beyond the end of the rod.

easy!

If you don't want to bother with buttons for the banner finials, put a dollop of Scribbles paint at the end of the banner rod and round it with a toothpick.

finishing the tree banner stocking

1. Outline the star with Scribbles.

2. "Hang" the hearts from the trees. Refer to "Hanging Loops" on page 11.

3. Refer to "Getting It Together: Finishing Up" on pages 41–45.

finishing the angel banner stocking

1. With the ⅛″ ribbon, tie a bow and stitch it in place at the angel's neck. Refer to "Making Bows" on page 10.

2. Cut a 12″ piece of hair. Fold it in half and then in half again. Twist it once in the center. Refer to the angel banner pattern on the pullout at the back of the book for hair placement. With the glue gun, attach the center of the hair (where the twist is) to the top of her head. "Arrange" the hair and glue or stitch it in place.

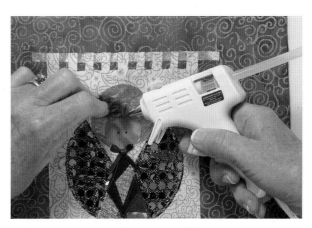

Attaching the angel's hair

3. Using Scribbles, put small dots on the dress for buttons and outline the heart in her hand. Refer to "Scribbles Paints" on pages 9–10.

4. Refer to "Getting It Together: Finishing Up" on pages 41–45.

fun!

Instead of ribbon, put "pearls" on the angel. Buy these at a craft shop and attach them with the glue gun or a couching stitch.

poinsettia
stocking

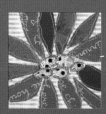

I painted watercolor poinsettias for Christmas cards one year. To make this design, I enlarged one of the cards a number of times and fiddled with it until it fit the stocking pattern. Either red or white poinsettias make a showy stocking.

What You'll Need

Refer to the main supply list on page 8 for the basics and add the following:

- ☐ 4 different whites (reds) for the bracts: ⅛ yard each*

- ☐ 5 greens, from lighter to darker, for the leaves: ⅛ yard each*

- ☐ White removable marker

- ☐ Piece of tissue paper

*Remember! Use your stash of scraps wherever ⅛-yard requirements are listed.

How-Tos

cutting

1. Refer to "Create the Pattern" on page 9 and follow the instructions.

2. Fold the stocking-body fat quarter in half and place it on a single layer of stabilizer. Pin the stocking pattern on top and cut it out.

the pattern

Trace the poinsettia pattern and stocking outline on the pullout at the back of the book onto tissue paper. Be sure to transfer the pattern letters and numbers. Cut it out on the stocking line.

appliqués

Refer to page 8 for instructions on using paper-backed fusible web. *Don't forget your pressing cloth.*

Use the reversed patterns on the pullout at the back of the book. Be sure to include the pattern letters and numbers when tracing. Trace the pattern pieces onto paper-backed fusible web in the following groups:

Poinsettia Stocking,
made by Franki Kohler,
2004

Poinsettia Stocking,
made for Betsy Reinhardt,
2004

poinsettia stocking **19**

1. Trace all the stems and leaf A and fuse them to the darkest green fabric.

2. Trace leaves B, C, and D and fuse them to 3 different medium green fabrics.

3. Trace leaves E and F and fuse them to the lightest green fabric.

4. Trace the oval centers and fuse them to a sequined or lamé fabric.

5. Trace flower bracts 1, 3, 7, 10, 11, 12, and 17 and fuse them to one white (red) fabric.

6. Trace flower bracts 6, 8, 9, 16, 18, and 20 and fuse them to one white (red) fabric.

7. Trace flower bracts 4, 5, 13, and 19 and fuse them to one white (red) fabric.

8. Trace flower bracts 2, 14, 15, and 21 and fuse them to one white (red) fabric.

9. Cut out all the appliqués on the pattern lines.

fun!

If you like beading, you could bead the flower centers.

fun!

Change the look of a fabric by sewing across the top of it with metallic thread. Zigzag stitch lines about ¼˝ apart or combine zigzag stitching with other plain or fancy stitches.

construction

1. Place the stocking front, which has the *toe pointing to the left*, right side up on the ironing board. Pin the tissue-paper pattern to the top edge.

2. Lift the paper pattern and position the 4 stems. Fuse them in place.

3. Position flower bracts 1–12 on the top flower and fuse them in place.

4. Position leaves A–F and fuse them in place.

5. Position flower bracts 13–21 on the bottom flower and fuse them in place.

6. Position and fuse the oval centers in place.

finishing

1. Use the pattern for reference and draw with the removable marker small stems that connect the leaves to the main stem. Draw in the leaf veins.

2. Pin the stabilizer to the back of the stocking. Use a straight stitch and metallic thread to machine stitch the stems and leaf veins. Finally, machine stitch around the very edge of the leaves, the flower bracts, and the main stems.

3. With Scribbles, paint around the oval flower centers. Set the piece aside to dry.

4. Refer to "Getting It Together: Finishing Up" on pages 41–45.

"Santa's been here" stocking

A pieced background adds interest to a stocking; if you're *very* ambitious, you can piece the stocking back as well. The placement of appliqués on these stockings is subjective. Place a heart here, an ornament there, a gift here or maybe there…It's *your* work of art!

"Santa's Been Here" Stocking,
made for Judy Spangenberg,
2004

"Santa's Been Here"
Stocking, made for
Amanda Gurr, 2004

What You'll Need

The instructions are for the dark blue stocking background. To make the silver background, substitute silver and gray fabrics for the dark blues, substitute silver rickrack for the gold, and eliminate the cotton batt.

Refer to the main supply list on page 8 for the basics and add the following:

☐ A variety of dark blues for the stocking background: 5″ × 12″ or ¼ yard each

☐ Reds, greens, creams, Christmas fabrics, gold lamé, and/or sequined fabrics for the tree and gifts: ⅛ yard each*

☐ Medium brown for the tree trunk: ⅛ yard*

☐ Muslin for the "Merry Christmas" sign: 3″ x 3″

☐ ⅛″-wide ribbon in red, green, gold, and/or silver, with or without a wired edge: 6″ per bow

☐ Gold narrow rickrack: ½ yard

☐ Cotton batt for snowbanks: 6″ x 6″

☐ Sharpie Ultra-Fine Point pen or a Pigma micron pen .05: black

☐ Removable transparent tape

***Remember! Use your stash of scraps wherever ⅛-yard requirements are listed.**

To save time, use a solid background.

How-Tos

Paper Piecing the Background

1. Trace the paper-piecing stocking body pattern onto a piece of pattern paper. Transfer the numbering. Use the patterns on the pullout at the back of the book. Cut them out.

2. To turn the finished stocking toe to the left, make the paper-piecing pattern, tape it to your light box or a window, and copy the lines from the opposite side. Use *this* side to paper-piece the background.

3. Cut scraps into the sizes needed to paper piece each section. See page 12 for paper-piecing instructions.

4. Paper piece the stocking. *Leave the paper on to serve as a cutting guide.*

Paper Piecing the Tree

1. Trace the tree paper-piecing pattern on the pullout at the back of the book onto pattern paper. Transfer the numbers.

2. Use a variety of plain, print, or sparkly scraps to paper piece the tree. Don't trim the edges, but do remove the paper.

cutting

1. Place the pieced stocking front and the fat quarter for the stocking back right sides together on top of a single layer of stabilizer. Pin and cut out the 3 layers on the paper-piecing pattern line.

2. Remove the paper-piecing pattern from the stocking front.

appliqués

Refer to page 8 for instructions on using paper-backed fusible web. *Don't forget your pressing cloth.*

Tree and Gifts

Use the tree, trunk, star, and snowbank patterns on the pullout at the back of the book. The remaining appliqué pieces can be drawn and cut freehand.

1. Trace the tree pattern onto paper-backed fusible web and fuse it to the tree fabric.

2. Trace the tree trunk onto paper-backed fusible web and fuse it to the tree trunk fabric.

3. Trace the star pattern onto paper-backed fusible web and fuse it to the gold lamé or sequined fabric.

4. Trace the snowbank patterns onto paper-backed fusible web and fuse them to the 6″ × 6″ square of batting.

5. Cut out all the appliqué shapes on the pattern lines.

6. Fuse small pieces of paper-backed fusible web (about 2″ squares) to a variety of scraps, including a lamé and a sequined fabric. Cut out squares and rectangles for the gifts, varying the sizes. Cut out hearts, bells, ornaments, candy canes, or Christmas stockings for the bottom of the tree.

easy!

If you have scraps of fabric with fusible web left over from another project in the book, use these.

"Merry Christmas" Signs

There are 2 signs with 2 backgrounds. Use removable tape to hold your muslin in place on the pattern.

1. Spray starch and press both sides of the 3″ × 3″ muslin fabric.

2. Center the muslin over the lettering pattern; tape it down. Use the Merry Christmas lettering pattern on the pullout at the back of the book.

3. Copy the lettering onto the muslin using a permanent ink pen.

4. Fuse the muslin to paper-backed fusible web.

5. Cut out each word with about a $3/16''$ margin all around. The cuts don't have to be exact.

6. Fuse the words to the fabrics you want to use for backgrounds.

7. Fuse the backgrounds to paper-backed fusible web.

8. Cut out each word with its background. My "Merry" is $1\frac{5}{8}'' \times 1''$ and "Christmas" is $2\frac{1}{4}'' \times 1''$.

easy!

If you want to make just one sign, write "Merry" and "Christmas" together.

construction

1. Place the stocking background on the ironing board. Place the tree trunk first, putting one snowbank behind the trunk. Then place the tree, "Merry Christmas" signs, and star. Remember to account for the stocking seam allowance. Press all of this into place.

2. Add more snowbanks; be sure to put one *over* the bottom of the tree trunk. When you've covered the entire bottom area of the stocking, press these into place.

3. Pile up the gifts. Position the pieces that are to hang from the bottom of the tree about $1/4''$ beneath it. Press.

4. Cut a $2''$, a $3''$, a $4''$, and a $5''$ piece of rickrack. Place these on the tree between the A, B, C, and D points. The rickrack should be wider than the tree and can either droop or not. Pin the rickrack to hold it in place.

5. Pin the stabilizer to the back of the stocking.

Machine stitch around the tree, trunk, star, gifts, and signs with metallic thread and a straight stitch. Trim excess rickrack close to the edge of the tree.

finishing

1. "Hang" the appliqués beneath the tree. Refer to "Hanging Loops" on page 11.

2. Make and attach a variety of bows to the gifts. See "Making Bows" on page 10–11.

3. The hearts on the tree are not pressed down, but hang freely. To make these double-sided hearts: Cut 2 rectangles $1\frac{1}{2}'' \times 4''$ each from sequined and/or lamé fabric. Fuse paper-backed fusible web to one rectangle. Place the webbed side on the wrong side of the other rectangle and press. Cut out 5 hearts. Thread a needle with metallic thread and knot the end. Come up through the back of the stocking and the lower edge of the rickrack (point A). Leaving about $3/8''$ of thread free between the tree and the heart, come up through the bottom of the heart's "V" (point B) and take a tiny stitch through point C. Repeat the stitch between B and C. Put the needle back through the stocking at point A and tack the thread down on the stocking back.

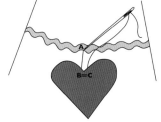

Hanging double-sided hearts

fun!

Instead of hearts, cut out double-sided Christmas ornaments in circles, diamonds, or ovals.

4. Outline the star with Scribbles. See "Scribbles Paints" on pages 9–10.

5. Refer to "Getting It Together: Finishing Up" on pages 41–45.

partridge stocking

My *Partridge Stocking* is made on a paper-pieced background, but the stocking is just as elegant with a wholecloth background. While this design looks complicated, it is not hard to put together.

What You'll Need

Refer to the main supply list on page 8 for the basics and add the following:

- ☐ A variety of white and gold fabrics for stocking background: ⅛ yard each*

- ☐ Black fabric for the partridge's head: ⅛ yard*

- ☐ Mottled or dotted fabric for the partridge breast: ⅛ yard*

- ☐ Fabric for the wings: ⅛ yard*

- ☐ Dark brown fabric for the tree trunk: fat quarter

- ☐ 6 green fabrics in varying shades for the leaves: ⅛ yard*

- ☐ Red lamé for the berries: ⅛ yard*

- ☐ Gold lamé for the pears: ⅛ yard*

- ☐ 10 red beads for the berries

- ☐ 1 blue or green bead for the partridge's eye

- ☐ Removable marker

- ☐ Piece of tissue paper

*Remember! Use your stash of scraps wherever ⅛-yard requirements are listed.

How-Tos

Paper Piecing the Background

1. Trace the paper-piecing stocking body pattern on the pullout at the back of the book onto a piece of pattern paper. Transfer the numbering.

2. To make the toe point left, place the pattern face down on a light box or tape it to a window, and redraw the exact pattern on the back of it. *This is the side of the paper-piecing pattern you will work from; be sure to make a note of that on the pattern paper.*

3. Cut scraps into the sizes needed for paper piecing each section. See page 12 for paper piecing instructions.

4. Paper piece the stocking. *Leave the paper on for a cutting guide.*

cutting

1. Place the pieced stocking front and the fat quarter for the stocking back right sides together on top of a single layer of stabilizer. Pin and cut out the 3 layers on the paper-piecing pattern line.

Partridge Stocking, made for Christina Doak, 2004

Alternate *Partridge Stocking,* made by Franki Kohler for Ron Cutting, 2004

2. Remove the paper-piecing pattern from the stocking front.

the pattern

Trace the partridge pattern and stocking outline on the pullout at the back of the book onto tissue paper. Be sure to transfer the letters and numbers. Cut it out on the stocking line.

appliqués

Refer to page 8 for instructions on using paper-backed fusible web. *Don't forget your pressing cloth.*

fast!

To make my stocking, I took a number of green scraps and ironed paper-backed fusible web to them. Then I cut my leaves freehand. You could do the same.

1. Use the reversed patterns on the pullout at the back of the book. Trace the leaf pattern pieces onto paper-backed fusible web in the following groups. Be sure to transfer the pattern numbers. After tracing, cut out each group as a section and fuse them to a green fabric:

Leaves 2, 6, 15, 19, 26, and 33.
Leaves 7, 11, 17, 23, 28, and 32.
Leaves 5, 9, 12, 16, 22, and 24.
Leaves 1, 10, 20, 27, and 29.
Leaves 3, 13, 14, 21, and 30.
Leaves 4, 8, 18, 25, and 31.

2. Trace the pears (patterns A and B) and fuse them to gold lamé.

3. Trace 10 berries (pattern G) and fuse them to red lamé.

4. Trace the tree trunk and branches (pattern H) and fuse them to a dark brown fabric.

5. Trace the partridge head (pattern C) and fuse it to black fabric.

6. Trace the partridge body (pattern D) and fuse it to mottled or dotted fabric.

7. Trace the wings (patterns E and F) and fuse them to wing fabric. *Note:* If the wing fabric is directional, slightly tilt patterns E and F so that the design direction isn't going *exactly* the same way.

8. Cut out all the appliqués on the pattern lines.

construction

1. Place the stocking front right side up on the ironing board. Pin the tissue paper pattern to the top edge.

2. Lift the paper pattern and position the trunk. Press it into place.

3. Position the pears and leaves and press them into place.

4. Position and press the partridge pieces in this order: C, D, E, and F.

5. Position the berries on the lower left and press them into place.

6. Position one berry at the tip of the partridge's beak and press it into place.

finishing

1. Using the pattern for reference, draw with a removable marker the small stems connecting the main stem to the leaves. Draw in the berry stems. Draw in the partridge's legs and feet.

2. Pin the stabilizer to the back of the stocking. Use a straight stitch and metallic thread to machine stitch around the very edge of the leaves, trunk, branches, partridge, and pears. Machine stitch the stems, partridge legs, and feet.

3. Sew a red bead at the end of each berry. Sew a bead for the partridge's eye.

4. Refer to "Getting It Together: Finishing Up" on pages 41–45.

patchwork stockings

This is one of my favorite stockings, because nothing I sew on a machine comes out with matched points, and in this design, the point is to leave the points unmatched. It's a great stocking for a child or adult, and you can use the background with a number of different themes.

The instructions that follow are for the *Gifts Stocking* in blues, greens, and white. To make the *Candy Cane Stocking*, substitute red scraps for blue and add a red-and-white striped fabric (for the candy canes) to the list below. You won't need the reds, greens, lamés, and sequined fabrics for the gifts. A pattern for the candy cane is on the pullout at the back of the book; the hearts are cut freehand.

What You'll Need

Refer to the main supply list on page 8 for the basics and add the following:

☐ A variety of white/cream fabrics for patchwork: ¼ yard each

☐ A variety of blue and green fabrics for patchwork: ⅛ yard each*

☐ Reds, greens, lamé, and sequined fabrics for the gifts: ⅛ yard each*

☐ ⅛″-wide ribbon in red, green, silver, and/or gold, with or without a wired edge: 6 ″ per bow

*Remember! Use your stash of scraps wherever ⅛-yard requirements are listed.

Candy Cane Stocking,
made for Greg Poulo,
2004

Gifts Stocking,
made for Patrick Terry,
2004

How-Tos

cutting

1. Refer to "Create the Pattern" on page 9 and follow the instructions.

2. Cut 30–35 rectangles 2½″ in length, ranging from 1″ to 2½″ wide from the blue, green, and white scraps.

3. Cut 1 rectangle 2″ × 5″ from a green or blue scrap for M.

4. Cut 3 squares 4½″ × 4½″ from a variety of white scraps for I, J, and K.

5. Cut 1 rectangle 5⅝″ × 5″ from a white scrap for L.

fun!

Instead of a gifts or candy cane design, substitute trees, stars, hearts, holly leaves, Christmas ornaments, bells, or reindeer.

Piecing the Background

1. Sew the 2½″ rectangles into strip units. For each strip unit, randomly vary the widths of the scraps. The stocking requires 7 strip units that are a *minimum* of 4″ wide (A to G).

2. Sew a strip unit that is a *minimum* of 6″ wide (H).

Note: Because you're using random widths, the strip units may turn out a bit wider than the minimum measurements. Don't bother to trim them.

3. Press all seams open.

easy!

To choose scraps at random, jumble them up in a pile. Close your eyes and pick up a piece. Use whatever you come up with, unless you've pulled the same fabric twice.

4. Arrange the units as shown in the illustration.

5. Sew the units into sections. Note the G and F are turned 90° before being stitched to L.

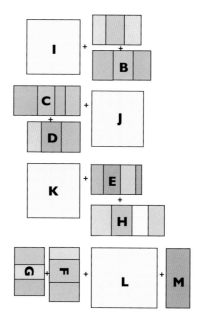

Piecing Diagram

6. Trim section I/A/B to 4¼″ long.

7. Trim section C/D/J to 4″ long.

8. Trim section K/E/H to 4¼″ long.

9. Do not trim section G/F/L/M.

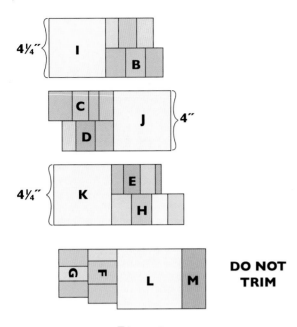

Trim sections.

DO NOT TRIM

10. Sew the 4 sections together, slightly offsetting each section to avoid a vertical center seam. Press the seams open.

11. Place the stocking pattern on the pieced background. The background should be larger than the pattern. If there's a shortfall of fabric at any point, simply piece on another bit of fabric.

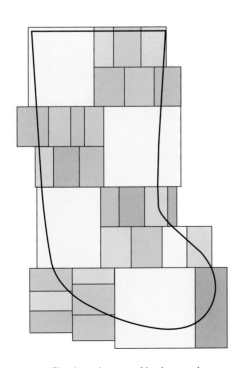

Checking the pieced background

cutting

Place the pieced stocking front and the fat quarter for the stocking back right sides together on top of a single layer of stabilizer. Pin and cut out the 3 layers on the pattern line.

appliqués

Refer to page 8 for instructions on using paper-backed fusible web. *Don't forget your pressing cloth.*

1. Choose a variety of scraps in reds, greens, dark blue, gold, or silver. These pieces don't need to be larger than 3″ to 4″ in length or width. Fuse them to paper-backed fusible web.

2. Cut rectangles and squares in different sizes and colors for the gifts.

construction

1. Place the stocking front on the ironing board and group the gifts in the large white areas of the stocking. Remember to account for the ¼″ seam allowance on the outside edge of the stocking.

2. When you are pleased with the gift arrangement, press the appliqués in place.

3. Pin the stabilizer to the wrong side of the stocking. Machine stitch around the gifts with metallic thread.

finishing

1. Make and attach a variety of bows to the gifts. See "Making Bows" on pages 10–11.

2. Refer to "Getting It Together: Finishing Up" on pages 41–45.

easy!

Save your leftover fused fabrics in a box to use on future projects. They're especially useful for the mini stockings.

stockings for elves:
mini stockings

At Christmas, hang these adorable minis on door handles, put them on the tree, tie them to the tops of presents, or give them as gifts.

The pattern for the mini stockings is made from freezer paper so the backgrounds can be cut without the fuss of pinning. The hanger can go on the front or the back. The toe can point either way. Cut the appliqués with or without patterns, and use a glue gun to attach the extras. What could be easier?

I know you'll love these, so the instructions below assume you'll be making more than one.

What You'll Need

- Whites, creams, reds, greens, dark blue, and/or Christmas fabrics for the stocking: ⅛ yard each*

- Gold lamé for the header and/or appliqués: ⅛ yard*

- Sequined fabric for the header and/or appliqués: ⅛ yard*

- Brown/black fabric for holly branches and/or tree trunks: ⅛ yard*

- Satin cording (rattail), gold rickrack, or ⅛″-wide ribbon in green, red, or gold for hangers: 1 yard for 5 stockings

- Freezer paper

- Paper-backed fusible web: ½ yard

- Small stars and hearts stickers for *Trees Stockings (page 37)*

- Glue gun

*Remember! Use your stash of scraps wherever ⅛-yard requirements are listed.

Mini stockings: *Candy Cane, Stars, Holly and Berries*

How-Tos

the pattern

Using the mini stocking pattern on the pullout at the back of the book, trace the outline of the stocking onto a piece of freezer paper and cut it out. Ignore the paper-piecing lines.

Paper Piecing the Background

You can make these stockings from a whole piece of fabric or you can make a pieced background from very small scraps. The pattern on the pullout at the back of the book allows you to do it either way. I've drawn paper-piecing lines on this pattern, but notice that my pieced backgrounds vary. Make one using the pattern and then draw your own lines. Refer to "Paper Piecing" on page 12. Cut the pattern on the lines and remove the paper. Go to Step 2 at right.

cutting

1. If you want the stocking toe to turn to the right, press the freezer-paper pattern to the right side of the background fabric. If you want the toe to turn left, press the pattern to the wrong side of the fabric. Cut around the pattern. Pull the pattern off and save it for reuse.

fast!

If you are mass-producing the stockings, get a number of backgrounds together at your ironing board to press and cut in one session. If you don't hold the iron on the freezer-paper pattern for more than 2–3 seconds, the pattern can be reused 25–30 times.

2. Cut 1 rectangle 3½" × 2¼" from the lamé, sequined, or Christmas fabric for the header. The basic header height is 2¼", but you may want to shorten or lengthen it. The width will still be 3½".

easy!

When working with lamé, avoid raveling by making all cuts on the bias.

3. Cut one 6½" piece of cording for the hanger. This size will fit over a standard doorknob.

appliqués

Refer to page 8 for instructions on using paper-backed fusible web. *Don't forget your pressing cloth.*

fun!

If your fabrics look a bit blah, sparkle them up. With a toothpick, scrape a thin layer of Scribbles over the top of the fabric. Or use Scribbles to paint swirls or curvy lines onto a piece of plain fabric.

1. Choose a variety of small scraps of red, green, Christmas, sequined, and lamé fabrics. Fuse paper-backed fusible web to the back of all these. Fuse a piece of paper-backed fusible web to a striped fabric for a candy cane stocking. If you are making the trees or holly designs, you'll need to fuse a piece of brown or black for the trunks/stems.

2. Optional: Piece together odds and ends of green, red, sequined, and lamé fabrics. Press the seams open and fuse paper-backed fusible web to the back. Cut out colorful hearts, trees, stars, leaves, and candles.

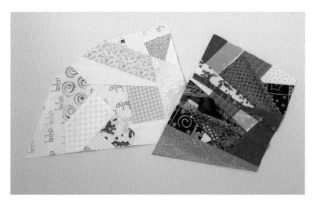

Piece odds and ends for interesting appliqués.

3. Pick the stocking you want to make and use it as a reference for the design. The candy cane appliqué pattern is on the pullout at the back of the book. For the other stockings, cut the appliqués you need freehand.

construction

Remember to allow for the seam allowance when positioning the appliqués.

1. For the *Hearts* or *Stars* mini stockings, cut 2 pieces of ribbon and baste them into place on the stocking front. Cut the heart or star appliqués and press them into place, overlapping the bottom of the ribbons.

Baste ribbons for *Hearts* mini stocking.

2. For the *Bells* mini stocking, cut a 4˝ piece of ⅛˝ ribbon. Drape this from side to side at the top of the stocking and baste it into place. Cut the bells and position them at different heights below the ribbon. Press them into place.

3. For the other stockings, cut the appliqués and press them into place.

fast!

I don't bother with a stabilizer when stitching these small stockings. Instead, I use a piece of paper under the background and tear it off when I'm finished.

fun!

To make bell clappers, cut small circles from your fused leftovers. Or make them from beads, buttons, or tiny jingle bells.

fun!

If you have any raffia around, use it for a stocking hanger or to hang the bells, stars, or hearts.

finishing

1. Machine stitch around the edges of the appliqués or paint the edges with Scribbles. See "Scribbles Paints" on page 9. You can also leave them plain.

2. Make bows for gifts, hearts, candles, candy canes, bells, or stars mini stockings. See "Making Bows" on page 10.

3. "Hang" bells or other decorations on the bottom of the trees. See "Hanging Loops" on page 11.

assembling the mini

1. Center the header piece on the stocking top; pin and sew it. Trim it to fit the stocking.

2. Fold the lining fabric right sides together. Place the fabric for the stocking back *wrong* side up on top of the lining piece.

3. Place the stocking front *right* side up on this package and pin it. Cut out all the layers using the stocking as a pattern.

4. Place the stocking hanger so the raw edges are even with the stocking *front or back*. Position the

mini gallery

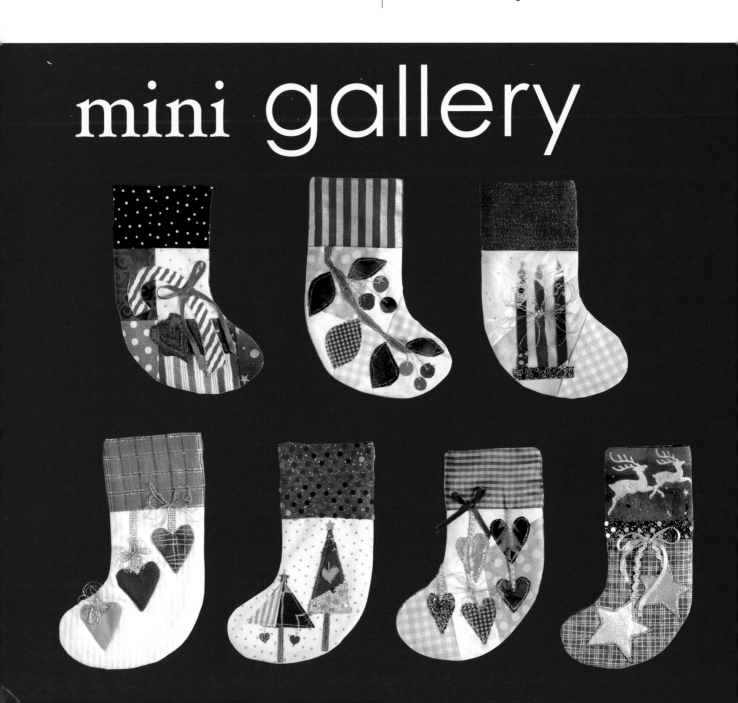

cording ⅜″ from the stocking top edges, with the loop hanging down. Baste it into place.

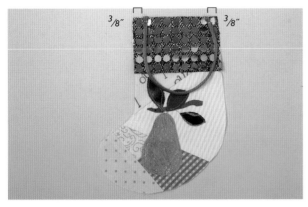

Position and baste the hanger.

5. With right sides together, sew the stocking front to the lining along the top edge. Press the seam toward the lining.

6. Repeat Step 5 with the stocking back. Press the seam toward the back.

7. Push the cording toward the inside of the stocking and pin it down so you won't sew it into the side seams. Pin the bows away from the seam allowance.

8. Mark a 1½″ opening on the straight seam of the heel side of the lining; this will not be sewn.

9. Refer to "Assembling the Stocking" on pages 44–45 to complete the stocking.

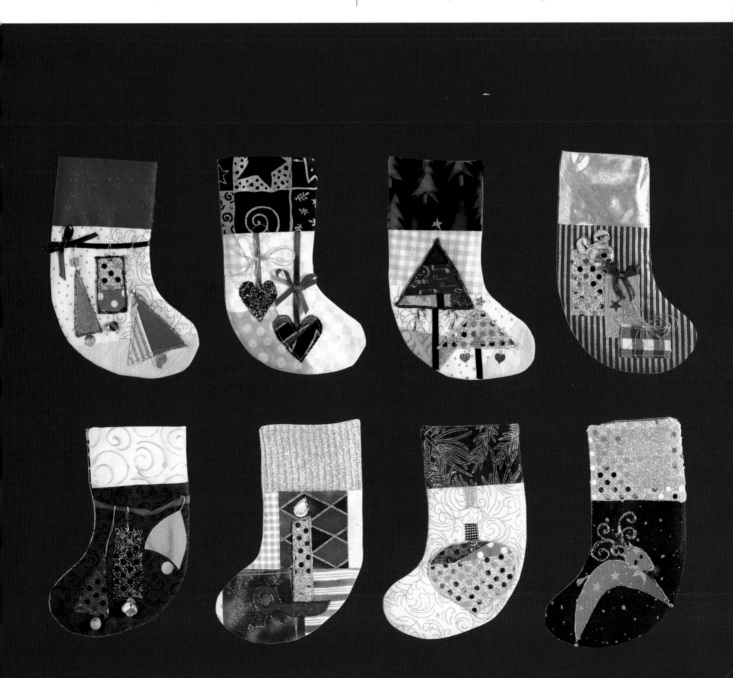

Santa,
Who Are You?
Making Labels

A stocking needs a label. When considering what to put on your stocking, ask yourself, "If I found a stocking in a trunk in my great-grandmother's attic, what would I want to know about it?" The simplest label includes the name of the stocking recipient, the date the stocking was made, and your name as the maker. If you want to add more, include the city and state where the stocking was made, the city and state where the recipient lives, and his or her relationship to you. If the stocking is for a child, you might add, for example, "Joe's Fifth Christmas." If this is a child's first Christmas, consider including the child's date of birth. You could also add a sentiment or apt quote, making the label its own gift.

I know that you can use a computer to produce a label, but I think of a label as a part of the total work, like an artist's signature—distinctive, personal, and part of the design. Instructions follow for the old-fashioned method of writing to fabric without technical support.

What You'll Need

- ☐ 6″ × 6″ square of muslin pressed on both sides with spray starch
- ☐ Ruled paper or plain paper with parallel lines drawn on it
- ☐ Permanent black pen (I use Pigma pens and Sharpie Extra-Fine or Ultra-Fine Point pens.)
- ☐ Iron and ironing board
- ☐ Light box (if you have one) or a Sharpie Extra-Fine Point pen
- ☐ Removable or drafting tape

easy!

You can use freezer paper to stabilize muslin for writing, but this adds another layer between the muslin and the master copy and makes the copy harder to see. Instead, use spray starch to stiffen the fabric.

easy!

A glass table with a light under it works well as a light box.

Label made for Emily Doak

Label made for Patrick Terry

Label made for Christina Doak

How-Tos

preparing the frame

easy!

> To improve your script, write slowly and enlarge your lettering.

You'll need a frame to help you produce a label that has level script and is correctly sized for the stocking.

If You Have a Light Box

1. Tape a piece of lined paper onto your light box or table.

2. Draw a vertical line 1″ in from the left edge (some lined paper already has this line). Add another vertical line 4″ to the right of the first line.

If You Don't Have a Light Box

Use a Sharpie pen to draw the lines above and then draw 3 or 4 horizontal lines about ⅜″ apart. If you're writing out a long label, add a few more lines.

make a master copy

You may write directly onto muslin or make a master copy to pre-edit your results before committing them to fabric. If you intend to wing it, the frame becomes your master copy. See "Write on Fabric" at right.

1. Write or print your information on your lined paper between the 2 vertical lines. If you don't have a light box, write with a Sharpie pen to ensure that you'll be able to see the master copy through the muslin.

2. If you're unhappy with the initial result, redo it. Once you're satisfied, this becomes your master copy.

3. When concentrating on attractive handwriting, even good spellers can get something wrong or leave out words. Be sure to proofread your master copy.

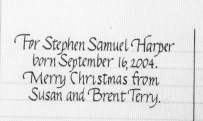

For Stephen Samuel Harper
born September 16, 2004.
Merry Christmas from
Susan and Brent Terry.

Master copy

write on fabric

1. Center and tape the piece of starched muslin over your master copy.

2. Use a permanent pen.

3. If you are writing directly onto fabric, use the ruled lines on the paper to keep your handwriting from veering off course. Stay within the vertical lines.

4. If you are using a written-out master copy, copy from this onto your fabric. For best results, don't re-pen what you've already written.

5. Press the label using steam to ensure permanence.

6. Use your rotary cutter and a clear ruler to trim the label, leaving a minimum ½″ margin outside the written or decorated edges.

7. Press under a ¼″ seam allowance.

fun!

> If you have red and green permanent pens, you can draw a motif on the label: try a holly leaf and berries or a Christmas tree. Or, if you want to go all out, use leftover pieces of fused fabrics to cut out stars, hearts, candy canes, or gifts. Press these to your label. Add bows to the gifts.

Getting It Together:
Finishing Up

Once you've finished the project instructions, refer to this section to assemble the stocking.

How-Tos

cutting

1. Cut 2 each of the header pattern from the header fabric and stabilizer for the headers.

2. Cut 2 strips, each 9″ × 1¼″, from sequined or lamé fabric for the divider strips.

3. Cut 1 strip 1½″ × 4¾″ from the background or header fabric for the hook.

decorate the headers

1. Trace the letters needed for a name onto paper-backed fusible web. Use the reverse alphabet on the pullout at the back of the book. A name with more than 6 letters may require reducing the size of the letters or using a nickname.

2. Cut out the letters as a section and press them to the wrong side of the lettering fabric. Cut out the letters.

easy!

When cutting small pieces move the *piece* you're cutting, not the scissors. My favorite scissors for this work are the 5″ sharp-pointed Fiskars sold in craft stores.

fun!

If you get tired of using my alphabet, go to the library or bookstore and find a book with additional alphabets in it. To reverse the letters, first copy the alphabet, enlarging it if necessary. Turn this paper over and tape it to a light table or window. Trace the letters with a Sharpie Extra-Fine Point pen.

3. Fold the header in half vertically and finger-press. Center the letters evenly on either side of the fold for a name with an even number of letters. For a name with an odd number of letters, center the middle letter on the fold. Using a clear ruler, check to see if the top and bottom margins are about equal. Press.

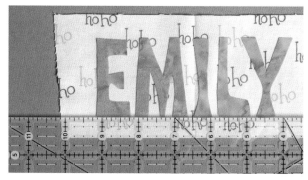

Check alignment of letters.

fun!

If you're working with a short name and want to add hearts or stars on either side, press fusible web to a piece of fabric, cut out the designs, and press them to your header.

4. If you're putting the year on the back header, repeat Steps 1–3.

5. Baste the stabilizer to the wrong side of the front and back headers ⅛″ from the edge on all sides.

6. Sew the letters (numbers) down or paint them with Scribbles.

Sew in place or paint.

construction

Before starting, make sure any area painted with Scribbles is dry.

1. Finger-press the center bottom of the front header section. Fold a divider strip in half and finger-press it. With right sides together, match the centers and pin the divider strip to the bottom edge of the header. Sew. The divider strip will be longer than the header on both ends. *Don't trim it yet!*

2. Finger-press the center top edge of the stocking front. With right sides together, match the stocking front center and divider strip center and sew.

3. Press the seam allowance toward the divider strip. *Don't forget your pressing cloth.*

4. Trim excess divider strip.

5. Repeat Steps 1–4 for the stocking back.

Trim divider strip.

make and attach the hook

1. Fold the hook fabric in half lengthwise and press.

2. Open the fabric. Fold the raw edges in to meet at the center crease and press.

Press the hook.

3. Fold lengthwise, matching the folded edges.

4. Sew ⅛″ from the double-folded lengthwise edge.

easy!

When pressing small pieces of fabric, put a glove on your "nonpressing" hand so you won't burn your fingers. Finger cots on your thumb, index, and middle fingers will also work.

5. Place the stocking back right side up. Fold the hook in half so the raw edges meet. On the *heel side* of the stocking, place the hook ⅜″ from the side edge of the stocking. Baste ⅛″ from the edge.

Hook position

cut and assemble the lining

1. Fold the lining fabric with right sides together and *smooth it out flat*. Pin the stocking front to the lining. Cut the lining at the exact edge of the stocking front so it will not be larger than the stocking.

2. With right sides together, sew the stocking front to the lining along the top edge. Press the seam toward the lining.

3. Repeat Step 2 for the stocking back, pressing the seam toward the stocking back.

4. To prevent the hook from being sewn into the seam, push it toward the middle of the stocking back and pin it in place. On the stocking front, pin aside any bows or tails of bows that may overlap the seam allowance.

Pin hook away from seam.

5. If you have a label, center it 1″ down from the top of the back lining and stitch it in place.

Label placement

6. With right sides together, pin the stocking front and back together, matching the header and divider strips.

7. Pin the lining front and back together.

8. On the heel side of the lining and 3″ down from where the lining meets the stocking, mark off a 5″ area that will not be sewn.

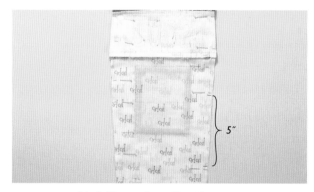

Mark 5″ area that will not be sewn.

assembling the stocking

Sew the stocking with a ¼″ seam allowance and the lining with a ⅜″ allowance to ensure that the lining will be slightly smaller than the stocking and will fit inside it smoothly.

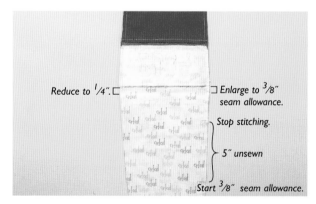

Seam allowances

easy!

I use an X-Acto knife for a seam ripper. The tip of the knife slips under a stitch and slits it neatly. When I am not using the knife, I push the blade into an old wine cork.

1. Set the sewing machine to 20 stitches per inch. *This is important!*

2. Using the previous photo as a guide, start sewing the lining at the bottom of the open area. Sew a $\frac{3}{8}$″ seam around the bottom of the lining and up the lining front. At 1″ from where the lining meets the stocking, taper down to a $\frac{1}{4}$″ seam. Sew the entire stocking with a $\frac{1}{4}$″ seam. As soon as you reach the lining again, graduate the seam to $\frac{3}{8}$″ and sew to the stop line.

3. Check the seam on the stocking to be sure the curves are smooth. Resew any area that has "points."

4. Place the lining on the ironing board and press the unsewn seam allowance back toward the wrong side of the lining. Do this on both the front and back lining.

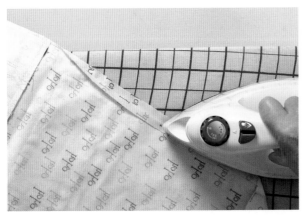

Press unsewn seam allowance.

trim, clip, and press

1. Trim the seam allowances in all curved areas of the stocking to $\frac{1}{16}$″. *Except for the unsewn area*, trim the remainder of the stocking and all of the lining seam allowances to $\frac{1}{8}$″.

2. Turn both the stocking and the lining to the right side. Press the *stocking* only.

3. On the right side of the lining, at the edge of the pressed-under seam allowance in the unstitched area, machine stitch the lining together.

4. Push the lining into the stocking and press the top of the stocking.

5. Sit back and admire your handiwork!

easy!

If a stocking has ribbon bows and the final pressing process has flattened them, roll a scrap of fabric into a tube, put this inside the bow loop, and carefully press the loop to remove the crease.

A. *Hidden Hearts Forest Stocking*, made for Emma Stumpf, 1999

B. *Night Flight Stocking*, made for Jessica Stumpf, 1999

C. *Angel With Red Ribbon Stocking*, made for Louisa Stumpf, 2001

D. *Little Hearts Stocking*, made for Emily Doak, 2003

E. *Angel in the Sunset Stocking*, made for Halley Terry, 1999

F. *Birdhouse Stocking*, made for Katy Doak, 2004

G. *"Here Comes Santa Claus" Stocking*, made for Joe Gurr, 1999

H. *"Here Comes Santa Claus" Stocking*, made for Jack Gurr, 1999

I. *Angel in a Cloud Stocking*, made for Katy Doak, 1999

J. *Millennium Banner Stocking*, made for Katy Doak, 2000

K. *"Santa's Been Here" Stocking*, made for Emily Doak, 2004

L. *Fireplace Stocking* (with removable mini stocking hung from the "fireplace"), made for Katy Doak, 2003

M. *Santa on the Rooftop Stocking*, made for Katy Doak, 2002

N. *Little Hearts Stocking*, made for Katy Doak, 2001

About the Author

Photo by Jonathan Payne

Susan Terry made her first quilt at age five, after which she unfortunately got sidetracked into a college major in English, a family, and a job in computer programming. Happily, in 1990 she effected an escape from reality and a return to quilting.

After hand piecing her first large quilts, Susan discovered needle-turn appliqué. She has created a number of award-winning quilts in this medium, most of them her own designs and all of them hand quilted. Susan also designs and makes handmade cards.

This Christmas stocking obsession is a detour into which she wandered during one of her many attempts to use up fabric scraps. She's run out of grandchildren for whom to make stockings and is rapidly working her way through her extended family and friends. Soon she will have to find another use for all those tiny bits of fabric cluttering her workroom in Oakland, California.

Sources

For materials and tools mentioned in this book, check your local quilt shop or try the following mail-order sources.

Superior Threads

www.superiorthreads.com

For general quilting supplies:

Cotton Patch Mail Order 3405 Hall Lane, Dept. CTB
Lafayette, CA 94549 (900) 835-4418 (925) 283-7883
Email: quiltusa@yahoo.com Website: www.quiltusa.com

**For a list of other fine books by C&T Publishing,
write for a free catalog:**

C&T Publishing, Inc. P.O. Box 1456 Lafayette, CA 94549
(800)284-1114 Email: ctinfo@ctpub.com
Website: www.ctpub.com